W9-BJN-521

THE
IRISH SETTER

by Charlotte Wilcox

Consultant:
Shirley Farrington, President
Irish Setter Club of America

CAPSTONE
HIGH/LOW BOOKS
an imprint of Capstone Press
Mankato, Minnesota

Capstone High/Low Books are published by Capstone Press
818 North Willow Street • Mankato, MN 56001
http://www.capstone-press.com

Library of Congress Cataloging-in-Publication Data
Wilcox, Charlotte.
    The Irish setter/by Charlotte Wilcox.
        p. cm. — (Learning about dogs)
    Includes bibliographical references and index.
    Summary: An introduction to this hunting breed, known for its long
reddish-brown coat, covering its history, development, habits, and
required care.
    ISBN 0-7368-0006-9
    1. Irish setters—Juvenile literature. [1. Irish setters. 2. Dogs.] I. Title.
II. Series: Wilcox, Charlotte. Learning about dogs.
SF429.I7W55   1999
636.752'6—dc21

                                                                98-3748
                                                                    CIP
                                                                    AC

Editorial Credits
Matt Doeden, editor; Timothy Halldin, cover designer; Sheri Gosewisch,
    photo researcher
Photo Credits
Kent & Donna Dannen, 6, 8, 12, 16, 25, 28, 30, 32, 34
Mark Raycroft, cover, 4, 15, 19, 20, 26, 40
Unicorn/John Ebling, 10, 37, 39
UPI/Corbis-Bettmann, 22

Contents

Quick Facts about the Irish Setter

Description

Height: Male Irish setters stand about 27 inches
                 (69 centimeters) tall. Females stand about
                 25 inches (64 centimeters) tall. Height is
                 measured from the ground to the withers.
                 The withers are the tops of the shoulders.

Weight: Male Irish setters weigh about 70 pounds
                 (32 kilograms). Females weigh about
                 60 pounds (27 kilograms).

Physical features: Irish setters are tall and slender. They have straight, silky coats. The hair on the head is short. It is long on the ears, tail, and lower body.

Colors: Irish setters are red-brown. Some have a small white spot on the head, neck, or feet.

Development

Place of origin: Irish setters came from Ireland.

History of breed: Early Irish setters were red and white hunting dogs.

Numbers: The American Kennel Club registers about 2,300 Irish setters each year. Register means to record a dog's breeding record with an official club. The Canadian Kennel Club registers between 200 and 300 Irish setters each year.

Uses

Some owners enter Irish setters in dog shows. The dogs compete for prizes. Hunters use Irish setters to find birds. Irish setters also make good family pets.

Chapter 1

Playful Irish Setters

Irish setters are famous for their beautiful coats. Irish setters have long, silky coats. Their coats are usually red-brown.

Irish setters are among the most playful of dog breeds. They are curious and have a lot of energy. These features often get Irish setters into trouble. People must be very patient when they train Irish setters. But many people think Irish setters are worth the extra effort.

Setters

Irish setters are members of a group of hunting dogs called setters. A setter is a

Irish setters have long, silky coats.

hunting dog that can point its body toward a bird. The Irish setter is the most common of the setter breeds. Other setter breeds include English setters and Gordon setters.

Hunters value Irish setters for the dogs' hunting abilities. Irish setters have keen senses. They can smell and hear birds better than people can.

Some people admire Irish setters for the dogs' good looks. Most people like Irish setters because the dogs are so playful.

Some people value Irish setters for the dogs' good looks.

Chapter 2

The Beginnings of the Breed

Irish setters came from Ireland. Irish people bred these dogs to be good hunters. Hunters wanted large, fast dogs with a good sense of smell. Hunters wanted dogs that were good at spotting and pointing at birds.

Spaniels

Most people believe Irish setters came from spaniels. A spaniel is a short dog with wavy fur. Spaniels have long coats and long ears. They are very active dogs.

Most people believe Irish setters came from spaniels.

Irish setters are the largest of the setter breeds.

Spaniels came to England from Spain more than 600 years ago. Some spaniels were good at finding birds in bushes or tall grass. The spaniels pointed with their bodies to show the hunters where the birds were.

Some spaniels were better at pointing than others. Breeders crossed these spaniels with other pointing breeds to produce setters. They produced three breeds of setters. Irish setters were the largest of the setter breeds.

Hunting

Irish setters walked through the woods with hunters. The dogs froze in a special position whenever they sensed a bird. Irish setters pointed their noses toward birds and their tails straight out. They lifted up one of their front legs. They stood perfectly still in this position. Hunters call this position a set or a point.

Hunters watched their Irish setters as the dogs walked through the woods. Hunters knew birds were nearby when dogs pointed. Hunters used nets to capture the birds.

Red Setters

The first Irish setters were many colors and sizes. Hunters did not care about dogs' colors. They only wanted good hunting dogs.

Breeders allowed only the best hunting dogs to have puppies. Breeders looked for large, fast dogs. They wanted the dogs to pass these features to their puppies.

By the 1700s, color patterns began to appear in Irish setters. Many setters in Ireland were white with red patches. Some were all red.

Irish setters that were all red became popular during the early 1800s. The Earl of Enniskillen raised red setters. Enniskillen is a town in Northern Ireland. The earl's setters became popular with Irish people. His dogs had many puppies. These dogs passed on their coloring to their puppies. These puppies found homes with many Irish families.

Irish setters that were all red became popular during the early 1800s.

Chapter 3

The Development of the Breed

Most Irish setters of the 1800s were red and white. But this changed when people began to enter Irish setters in dog shows. Dog shows awarded prizes to dogs with the best appearance and training.

Dog shows began in England in 1859. Irish setters were very popular at the shows. Many Irish setters of the time had red and white coats. But the Irish setters that usually won dog shows were all red. Most people of the time thought red Irish setters were the most beautiful.

Many early setters such as this English setter had red and white coats.

Palmerston

One of the most famous Irish setters was Palmerston. He was born in Ireland in 1862. He had a dark red coat. Palmerston was larger than most setters. He weighed 64 pounds (29 kilograms). He was 23 and one-half inches (60 centimeters) tall.

Palmerston fathered many puppies. He passed his features to his puppies. Most of the puppies were dark red. They were larger than many other Irish setters. People brought several of Palmerston's puppies to North America. Most Irish setters in North America came from these dogs.

Some of Palmerston's sons and daughters appeared in North America's first dog show. The show was in Chicago, Illinois, in 1876. North Americans began breeding Irish setters soon after the first show. The breed became popular right away.

Most Irish setters in North America today came from Palmerston's offspring.

Irish Setter Clubs

The Irish Red Setter Club began in 1882 in Dublin, Ireland. In 1890, club members wrote a breed standard. A breed standard is a document that describes how dogs of a breed should look. The club's standard became the standard for Irish setters worldwide.

Irish setters were among the first breeds registered in North America. The Irish Setter Club of America began in 1891. The club adopted the Dublin standard for its dogs. Today, the American Kennel Club registers about 2,300 Irish setters every year.

The Irish Setter Club of Canada began in 1949. The Canadian Kennel Club registers between 200 and 300 Irish setters every year.

Irish setters were among the first breeds registered in North America.

Chapter 4
The Irish Setter Today

In 1945, author Jim Kjelgaard (CHELL-gard) wrote the book *Big Red*. It was a story about a boy and his Irish setter. In 1962, Walt Disney Productions made the story into a movie called *Big Red*. Many people read the book and saw the movie. They wanted to have Irish setters of their own.

During the early 1970s, President Richard Nixon kept an Irish setter in the White House. He named his Irish setter King Timahoe. Timahoe is a town in Ireland. Nixon's family came from Timahoe. The popularity of the Irish setter breed grew during Nixon's years as president.

President Richard Nixon had an Irish setter named King Timahoe.

Appearance

Irish setters are tall and graceful. Male Irish setters stand about 27 inches (69 centimeters) tall. Females stand about 25 inches (64 centimeters) tall. Height is measured from the ground to the withers. The withers are the tops of the shoulders. Males weigh about 70 pounds (32 kilograms). Females weigh about 60 pounds (27 kilograms).

The Irish setter's coat is straight and silky. The fur on the head is short. The fur is longer on the ears, tail, and lower body. This long fur is called feathering.

Irish setters actually are red-brown. Most people just call them red. Some have a small white spot on the head, neck, or feet.

Kinds of Irish Setters

People place Irish setters into two main groups. These groups are hunting Irish setters and Irish setter show dogs. People breed

Irish setters have long fur on their ears, tails, and lower bodies.

People bred Irish setters to be good hunters.

hunting setters to be good hunters. They breed show dogs to look good at shows.

People often call hunting setters red setters. Red setters usually are smaller and faster than Irish setter show dogs. Their coats are shorter. Often their fur is light red.

Irish setter show dogs are large. Their coats are thick and longer than the coats of red setters. Irish setter show dogs usually have darker fur than red setters.

Field Trials

Owners sometimes bring their Irish setters to field trials. A field trial is a sporting contest for dogs. Irish setters must find birds during field trials. The field trials take place in large fields. The fields have trees, bushes, and tall grass.

People release birds such as quail and pheasants before trials begin. A judge then signals owners to release their dogs. The dogs search for birds. They use their keen sense of smell to find the birds.

Each owner and Irish setter work as a team. The dog points when it finds a bird. The hunter shoots a gun into the air. The shot announces that the dog has found a bird. Dogs win points based on how many birds they find.

Some Irish setters serve as companion dogs to older people.

Service Dogs

Some Irish setters are service dogs. They help
people who are disabled. Service dogs may
help people who are deaf. The dogs may show
the people when an alarm or telephone rings.
Service dogs also help people who are in
wheelchairs. The dogs turn on lights, open

doors, and pick up objects. Other Irish setters are companion dogs to older people.

One famous service dog was an Irish setter named Lyric. Lyric lived in Nashua, New Hampshire. Lyric's owner had a breathing problem. The owner had to wear a mask hooked up to an oxygen machine. Lyric's owner could not breathe at night without the oxygen.

One night in 1996, the oxygen mask came unplugged. Lyric's owner was sleeping. She stopped breathing. Trainers had taught Lyric what to do if this happened. The dog dialed 911 on the telephone.

Lyric barked when the police answered. The police checked where the call came from. They sent a rescue team to the address. The team rushed Lyric's owner to the hospital. Lyric's quick action saved the woman's life.

Chapter 5
Owning an Irish Setter

Irish setters make good family pets. They need a lot of exercise and opportunities to play. Irish setters can be troublesome if they do not receive obedience training. This training teaches an animal to obey commands.

Irish setter puppies are playful. They often make messes if their owners do not watch them carefully. The puppies do not grow to their full size as fast as puppies of most other breeds. This is one reason many people enjoy owning Irish setters.

Irish setters make good family pets.

Exercise

Exercise is important for an Irish setter. An Irish setter needs lots of exercise to stay healthy. But owners should not let Irish setters run loose.

A fenced yard is the best place for an Irish setter. The area should provide shelter and shade. It should give the dog room to run and to play. The fence must be tall enough to keep the dog from jumping over it.

Owners who do not have yards for their Irish setters must exercise their dogs daily. Owners must take Irish setters running or walking every day. The dogs should be on leashes.

Irish setters can be difficult to walk. They may pull hard on their leashes. They may want to go faster than their owners. Some people solve this problem by jogging with their Irish setters.

Irish setters are good pets for active people. They need the company of people. Irish setters

Owners must take Irish setters running or walking every day.

Owners must brush their Irish setters' hair.

seem to enjoy swimming, jogging, and riding in cars. Some seem to enjoy hunting birds with their owners.

Caring for an Irish Setter

Irish setters have long coats that need to be brushed daily. Owners may spend an hour each day brushing their Irish setters' coats. Owners must cut long hair between Irish setters' toes.

Owners must also cut hair that grows inside Irish setters' ears.

Irish setters often get muddy and dirty when they go outside. Many owners bathe their Irish setters once each week.

Owners should clean Irish setters' teeth and clip their nails. Irish setters' long, furry ears can get dirty. Owners should clean their dogs' ears at least once each month.

Owners must check Irish setters for ticks every day during warm weather. Some ticks carry illnesses. Irish setters spend much of their time outdoors. This gives ticks a chance to get in the dogs' fur. Owners also should check for fleas, lice, and mites. These tiny insects can live in a dog's fur.

Feeding an Irish Setter

The best diet for an Irish setter is dog food. Pet stores carry several forms of dog food. The most common forms are dry, semimoist, and canned. A grown Irish setter may eat one pound (.5 kilogram) or more of dry or semimoist food each day. It may eat three or more cans of canned food each day instead.

Irish setters need plenty of water. Owners should make sure their dogs can drink as often as they want. The dogs should drink at least three times each day.

Finding a Lost Dog

Owners should be sure their dogs have identification. Some owners hang tags with a name and address on their dogs' collars. Others give their dogs tattoos. These marks on the skin contain information about how to contact a dog's owner.

Some people have veterinarians place microchips under their dogs' skin. Veterinarians can scan these tiny chips in lost dogs. The microchips contain information about the dog and how to contact its owner.

Owners should make sure their dogs have identification.

Finding a Puppy

Irish setter clubs help people find puppies. They can give people the names of good breeders. They also find families for dogs who have lost their homes.

Good breeders do not sell Irish setters through pet stores. Most breeders warn people not to buy dogs at pet stores. These dogs often are unhealthy.

Some people find Irish setters at rescue shelters. Rescue shelters find owners for homeless dogs. They offer grown dogs for adoption. These dogs usually cost less than dogs from breeders. Many of them are already trained.

Irish setters are good for people who want active dogs. They are friendly and get along well with people.

Irish setter clubs help people find puppies.

Muzzle

Ear

Withers

Chest

Forequarters

Hindquarters

Tail

Hock

Quick Facts about Dogs

Dog Terms

A male dog is called a dog. A female dog is called a bitch. A young dog is a puppy until it is one year old. A newborn puppy is a whelp until it no longer depends on its mother's milk. A family of puppies born at one time is called a litter.

Life History

Origin:	All dogs, wolves, coyotes, and dingoes descended from a single wolflike species. Dogs have been friends of people since early times.
Types:	There are about 350 different dog breeds. Dogs come in different sizes and colors. Adult dogs weigh from two to 200 pounds (one to 91 kilograms). They stand from six to 36 inches (15 to 91 centimeters) tall.
Reproduction:	Dogs mature at six to 18 months. Puppies are born two months after breeding. An average litter is three to six puppies, but litters of 15 or more are possible.
Development:	Newborn puppies cannot see or hear. Their ears and eyes open one to two weeks after birth. They try to walk about two weeks after birth. Their teeth begin to come in about three weeks after birth.
Life span:	Dogs are fully grown at two years. They may live up to 15 years.

The Dog's Super Senses

Smell: Dogs have a strong sense of smell. Dogs use their noses even more than their eyes and ears. They recognize people, animals, and objects just by smelling them. They may recognize smells from long distances. They also may remember smells for long periods of time.

Hearing: Dogs hear better than people do. Dogs can hear noises from long distances. They also hear high-pitched sounds that people cannot hear.

Sight: Dogs' eyes are on the sides of their heads. They can see twice as wide around their heads as people can. Most scientists believe dogs cannot see colors.

Touch: Dogs enjoy being petted more than almost any other animal. They also can feel vibrations from approaching trains or the earliest stages of earthquakes.

Taste: Dogs cannot taste much. This is partly because their sense of smell is so strong that it overpowers their taste.

Navigation: Dogs often can find their way through crowded streets or across miles of wilderness without any guidance. This is a special ability that scientists do not fully understand.

Words to Know

breed standard (BREED STAN-durd)—a
document that describes how dogs of a breed
should look
field trial (FEELD TRYE-uhl)—a sporting
contest for dogs
obedience training (oh-BEE-dee-uhns TRAY-
ning)—teaching an animal to obey commands
register (REJ-uh-stur)—to record a dog's
breeding record with an official club
service dog (SUR-viss DAWG)—a dog trained
to help a person who is disabled
setter (SET-uhr)—a hunting dog that can point
its body toward a bird
spaniel (SPAN-yuhl)—a hunting dog with
wavy fur and long ears
tattoo (ta-TOO)—a mark on the skin
veterinarian (vet-ur-uh-NER-ee-uhn)—a
person trained to treat the sicknesses and
injuries of animals
withers (WITH-urs)—the tops of an animal's
shoulders

To Learn More

Driscoll, Laura. *All about Dogs and Puppies.* All Aboard Books. New York: Grosset & Dunlap, 1998.

Hansen, Ann Larkin. *Dogs.* Popular Pet Care. Minneapolis: Abdo & Daughters, 1997.

Rosen, Michael J. *Kids' Best Field Guide to Neighborhood Dogs.* New York: Workman, 1993.

You can read articles about Irish setters in *AKC Gazette, Bird Dog News, Dogs in Canada, Dog Sports, Field Trial, Gun Dog,* and *Pointing Dog Journal* magazines.

Useful Addresses

American Kennel Club
5580 Centerview Drive
Raleigh, NC 27606

Canadian Kennel Club
89 Skyway Avenue, Suite 100
Etobicoke, ON M9W 6R4
Canada

Irish Setter Club of America
16717 Ledge Falls
San Antonio, TX 78232-1808

Irish Setter Club of Canada
10325 Highway 43
Mountain, ON K0E 1S0
Canada

Internet Sites

Cyber-Pet
http://www.cyberpet.com

Irish Setter Club of America
http://www.onofrio.com/clubs/IRISH_
  SETTER_CLUB_OF_AMERICA

Irish Setter Club of Canada
http://www.achilles.net/~va3mgt

**North American Versatile Hunting Dog
  Association**
http://www.navhda.org

Pet Net
http://www.petnet.com

Index